STOCKING STUMPERS

TRIVIA EDITION

By **S. Claus**
with help from **Jack Kreismer**

Red-Letter Press, Inc.

STOCKING STUMPERS- Trivia Edition
Copyright ©1997 Red-Letter Press, Inc.
ISBN: 0-940462-55-9
All rights reserved
Printed in the United States of America

For information address Red-Letter Press, Inc.
P.O. Box 393, Saddle River, NJ 07458

ACKNOWLEDGMENTS

A Stocking Stumpers salute to Santa's "subordinate clauses":

Cover design and typography: **s.w.artz, inc.**

Illustrations: **Jack Kreismer, Sr.**

Editorial: **Ellen Fischbein and Geoff Scowcroft**

Contributors: **Angela Demers and Russ Edwards**

A Personal Message from Santa

'Twas the Night Before Christmas
and I left the North Pole
to bring to your stocking
a fresh lump of coal;
But St. Nick's got heart
and your sins weren't voluminous,
so I brought you a gift
in lieu of bituminous;
Now since you've escaped
my long list of lumpers,
I've left you instead
Santa's favorite, Stocking Stumpers.
Merry Christmas!

S. Claus

FIRST THINGS FIRST

1. What are the first names of the two storytelling Brothers Grimm?

2. Who's the first baseman in Abbott and Costello's "Who's on First?" routine?

3. True or false: Limousines are so called because the first one was built by two men, Charles Limous and Thomas Ines.

4. What U.S. president was the first to use electric lights on a Christmas tree?

5. Instituted in 1938, what was the first minimum hourly wage in the U.S.?
   a) 25 cents b) 50 cents c) 75 cents d) $1.00

ANSWERS

1. Jacob and Wilhelm

2. Who

3. False- the vehicle name comes from the area it was first built, the "Limousin" region of France.

4. Grover Cleveland, in 1895

5. A

LEFT, RIGHT, LEFT, RIGHT

6. Are all polar bears right-handed or left-handed?

7. Is it only right-handers or lefties who are permitted to play polo?

8. The names of Eng and Chang, the Siamese twins, mean "left" and "right" in English. Which was which?

9. "Mancinism"- does that describe a southpaw or a righty?

10. True or false: Michelangelo, Leonardo daVinci and Jack the Ripper were all lefties.

ANSWERS

6. Left-handed

7. Right-handers. Left-handers are forbidden because of the possibility of collisions.

8. Eng means "left" and Chang means "right".

9. Left-handedness

10. True

POTPOURRI

11. A "piscatologist" participates in what activity?
12. Who was the first cartoonist to depict Santa Claus in his red-suited image?
13. How many states in the U.S. have the letter "z" in their name?
14. What fine feathered friend, whose middle name is Fauntleroy, made his film debut in a 1934 cartoon called *The Wise Little Hen?*
15. Where would you commonly see letters in this order: ECNALUBMA?

ANSWERS

11. Fishing

12. Thomas Nast

13. Just one- Arizona

14. Donald Duck

15. On the front of an ambulance (It's reversed
    so that, when you look in your rear view
    mirror while driving, it reads as though it's
    spelled forward.)

I-OPENERS

The answers to each of these questions begin with the letter "i".

16. What English word has six "i's" in it?

17. On Tuesday, May 30, 1911 Ray Harroun won the inaugural race with a speed of 74.59 miles per hour. What race?

18. What was the name of the Presidential campaign song composed by Irving Berlin in 1952?

19. Do you remember the slogan for a Peter Paul candy bar?

20. It was called this name, then Persia, then this name again. What country is this?

21. What company was originally called the Computing-Tabulating-Recording-Company?

22. What is the fifth most populous country in the world?

ANSWERS

16. Indivisibility
17. The Indianapolis 500
18. *I Like Ike*
19. Indescribably delicious
20. Iran
21. IBM
22. Indonesia

SIGN LANGUAGE

23. Is a stop sign an octagon, square, rectangle or hexagon?

24. What does the following mean?

    _ _   ·   ·_·   ·_·   _·_ _
    _·_·   ····   ·_·   ··   ···   _   _ _   ·_   ···!

25. V̄ signifies what Roman numeral?

ANSWERS

23. An octagon

24. It's Morse Code for "Merry Christmas!"

25. 5,000- a dash line over a numeral multiplies
    the value by 1,000; hence, the V, which
    stands for five, becomes 5,000.

HORSEPLAY

26. Even horses have stage names. What was Bamboo Harvester better known as on television?

27. According to race regulations, what is the maximum amount of letters a horse's name can be?

28. At one time, there was a horse named Cilohocla racing on a track in Florida. For the longest time, the folks couldn't figure out the reason for the name. Can you?

29. What do Omaha, Spokane and Johnstown have in common?

30. The great race horse Man O' War lost only one race in his entire career. What was unusual about this upset?

ANSWERS

26. Mr. Ed

27. Eighteen (in order to fit on a racing program)

28. Spelled backwards, the horse's name reads "Alcoholic."

29. They are horses that each won the Kentucky Derby- Spokane in 1889, Omaha in 1935 and Johnstown in 1939.

30. Upset was the name of the horse that defeated Man O' War.

HOLIDAY HITS

Match the song with the recording artist.

31. *Blue Christmas*
32. *Jingle Bell Rock*
33. *The Little Drummer Boy*
34. *I Saw Mommy Kissing Santa Claus*
35. *Grandma Got Run Over by a Reindeer*
36. *The Christmas Song*
37. *White Christmas*

a) Nat King Cole
b) Harry Simeone Chorale
c) Elmo and Patsy
d) Bing Crosby
e) Bobby Helms
f) Elvis Presley
g) Jimmy Boyd

ANSWERS

31. F
32. E
33. B
34. G
35. C
36. A
37. D

WHO AM I?

38. A famous actor, I failed my first screen test because of big ears. I had a $5,000 bounty placed on me during World War II to any German flier who captured me, dead or alive. When I got out of the service June 12, 1944 my discharge papers were signed by U.S. Army Captain Ronald Reagan.

39. I was a volunteer fireman. I also introduced spaghetti to America, but you're more likely to know me as a former United States President whose face adorns the two-dollar bill.

40. I earned ten dollars for a famous poem I wrote (Hint: the title of it would later become the nickname of a pro football team). I did much of my writing with a cat perched on my shoulders. I died at the age of forty, October 7, 1849. On the same day, another poet, James Whitcomb Riley, was born.

ANSWERS

38. Clark Gable
39. Thomas Jefferson
40. Edgar Allan Poe (A Baltimorean, it was Poe's *The Raven* which was the reason for the NFL's Baltimore Ravens to be so named.)

COVER TO COVER

41. Who has appeared on the cover of *Sports Illustrated* the most often?

42. Who's the only person to appear on the cover of *TV Guide* three weeks in a row?

43. Who was the cover feature of *People* magazine's first edition in 1974?

44. Norman Rockwell illustrated 317 covers over a 47 year period for what magazine?

45. Who was *Time* magazine's first Man of the Year?

ANSWERS

41. Michael Jordan
42. Michael Landon, in 1991
43. Mia Farrow
44. *The Saturday Evening Post*
45. Charles Lindbergh, in 1927

NOT YOUR AVERAGE JOE

Santa will consider you Joe College if you can come up with the answers to the questions below, answers which are all people named Joe.

46. What heavyweight boxer, who defended his crown a record 25 times, once said about an opponent, "He can run, but he can't hide"?

47. 'Tis the season and my real name fits the occasion, Joe Yule, Jr. You know me better by my stage name. What is it?

48. Other than Warren Harding's dad, who is the only U.S. President's father to survive his son?

49. Who was the first Little League baseball player to play Major League Baseball?

50. What communist leader was born Iosif V. Dzhugashvili?

ANSWERS

46. Joe Louis
47. Mickey Rooney
48. Joe Kennedy
49. Joey Jay
50. Joseph Stalin

TEASER TIMEOUT

Santa can't resist including some brain teasers in Stocking Stumpers, *so take a timeout from the trivia toughies and try your hand at the puzzles below.*

51. What's in the middle of nowhere?

52. Add three letters to make the following complete: TNESSFF_ _ _.

53. What's unique about the following sentence? Bores are people that say that people are bores.

54. Jingles, Santa's top elf, decided to go on strike this year. Accordingly, he scrawled this message to the boss:

     PAID
     I'M
     WORKED

     Can you state Jingles' grievance?

55. How far can a reindeer walk into the woods?

ANSWERS

51. The letter "h"

52. TTO completes the countdown from ten to one.

53. It's a "pseudodrome"- a phrase in which the words read the same forwards and backwards.

54. I'm overworked and underpaid.

55. Halfway- after that, the deer's walking out.

THE GAMES PEOPLE PLAY

The game here is simple enough- match the hobbyist with the hobby.

56. Deltiologist   a) Cigar band collector

57. Spelunker   b) Trivia buff

58. Lepidopterist   c) Banknote collector

59. Notaphile   d) Postcard enthusiast

60. Bandophile   e) Moth and butterfly devotee

61. Spermologist   f) Cave explorer

ANSWERS

56. D
57. F
58. E
59. C
60. A
61. B

THE BIRDS AND THE BEES

62. Are bald eagles bald?

63. How many eyes does a bee have?

64. Are there more penguins found in Santa's neck of the woods or south of the equator?

65. What causes the buzzing sound that bees make?

66. What's the only bird that can fly backwards?

ANSWERS

62. No. Slicked-down white feathers on top of its head makes the eagle appear to be bald from a distance.

63. Five- three small eyes on the top of its head and two bigger ones in front

64. There are none at the North Pole. All seventeen varieties of penguins are found south of the equator, most in Antarctica.

65. The rapid up and down and back and forth movement of their wings

66. The hummingbird

WHO SAID IT?

67. "Santa Claus has the right idea- visit people once a year."
    a) Victor Borge b) Steve Martin c) Sally Field d) Marshall Field

68. "Two weeks before Christmas, I always think of a good present for
    someone but it has to be ordered three weeks in advance."
    a) Erma Bombeck b) Art Buchwald c) Andy Rooney d) Elfis Presley

69. "My kids love to get money for Christmas because it's always the
    right size."
    a) Donald Trump b) Ebenezer Scrooge c) Uncle Scrooge d) Uncle Miltie

70. "Never give below your taste level. Never say: 'Well, I think it's disgusting,
    but it's just the sort of thing she would like.'"
    a) Miss Piggy b) Miss Manners c) Ann Landers d) Emily Post

ANSWERS

67. A
68. C
69. D (Milton Berle)
70. B

POTPOURRI

71. What product was originally called "Little Short-Cake Fingers"?

72. BC 1234 is the home telephone number you would call if you were more than a stone's throw away from what famous TV and movie couple?

73. According to both French and Pennsylvania Dutch tradition, who is Bells Nichols?

74. A U.S. nickel is made up of how much copper?
    a) 0% b) 25% c) 50% d) 75%

75. The flag of Italy was designed by:
    a) Michelangelo b) Napoleon Bonaparte c) Mussolini d) Betsy Rossi

ANSWERS

71. Twinkies

72. Fred and Wilma Flintstone

73. Santa's brother

74. D (and the other 25% is made up of nickel)

75. B

CALLING ALL CARS

76. White is the preferred color of choice among automobile buyers in America. What color is second?

77. Why wasn't the Chevrolet Nova a popular car in Mexico?

78. Who was the first U.S. president to ride in a car?
a) William McKinley b) Theodore Roosevelt c) William H. Taft
d) Woodrow Wilson

79. The BMW, FIAT and MG- can you spell out these acronyms?

80. Vanity plates have given many celebrities a license to brag.
Here are a few: BORG 9, A1ANA2, and REDUCE.
Do you know who they belong(ed) to?

ANSWERS

76. Green

77. Nova means "won't go" in Spanish.

78. If you answered either A or B, you're right. Strictly speaking, William McKinley was the first to ride in a car. His first ride was also his last ride. It was in a hearse. The first president to actually drive a car was Teddy Roosevelt.

79. Bavarian Motor Works, Fabricana Italiana Automobile Torino (Italian Automobile Factory at Torino) and Morris Garage, respectively

80. In order, they are Ernest Borgnine, Lawrence Welk and Jack LaLanne.

THE FEAR OF IT

Combine the word with the phobia it describes.

81. Astraphobia
82. Cynophobia
83. Glossophobia
84. Musophobia
85. Logizomechanophobia

a) Fear of speaking in public
b) Fear of mice
c) Fear of computers (or machines)
d) Fear of dogs
e) Fear of lightning and thunder

ANSWERS

81. E
82. D
83. A
84. B
85. C

ODDS AND ENDS

The term "Odds" and/or "Ends" are involved in the questions and/or answers in this segment of Stocking Stumpers.

86. Demetrios George Synodinos was a real "Wizard of Odds". You knew him better by what trumped up name?

87. According to a Gallup Poll, if you're the average American, what are the odds that you will eat at a fast-food restaurant today?
    a) one out of 50 b) one out of 20 c) one out of 10 d) one out of 5

88. "God Bless Us, Every One!" is the end of what Christmas epic?

89. Including the end zone, how long is an NFL playing field?

90. What does the name "chop suey" mean?

ANSWERS

86. Jimmy the Greek
87. D
88. *A Christmas Carol* (said by Tiny Tim)
89. 120 yards
90. You guessed it- "odds and ends".

POTPOURRI

91. What ill-fated automobile model was named after Henry Ford's only child?

92. The Latin Christmas carol *Adeste Fidelis* translates to what English title?

93. What's the only public place where the U.S. flag is flown around the clock?

94. Can you name the three official languages of Switzerland?

95. Excluding the joker, if you added the total number of letters in the names of the cards (ace, two, three, four, etc.) in a full deck, what would that number total?

ANSWERS

91. The Edsel

92. *Oh Come All Ye Faithful*

93. The Capitol building in Washington, D.C.
    (The flags are only taken down
    when it's time to replace them with new ones.)

94. French, German and Italian

95. The same as the number of cards in the deck- 52

TRUE OR FALSE

96. In South American countries, setting off fireworks is a popular way of celebrating Christmas.

97. Abraham Lincoln was a licensed bartender.

98. The potato is a native food of Ireland.

99. *My Country 'Tis of Thee* is the tune of the British national anthem.

100. 7-UP soda got its name from the gambling game of craps.

ANSWERS

96. True

97. True- Lincoln was a co-owner of a saloon called "Berry and Lincoln" in Springfield, Illinois in 1833.

98. False- potatoes originated in Peru and were brought to Europe by explorers.

99. True

100. False- the "7" part stems from when it was created in 1929 and was first sold in seven ounce containers. The "UP" part came from the direction in which the bubbles moved.

HOLIDAY HO HOs

It's time for another trivia break. See if you can answer these groaners from Santa's social director, Henny Elfman.

101. How come Santa keeps bells on his bathroom scale?

102. Why are red and green the colors of Christmas?

103. The elves love this one: What's another name for Santa's helpers?

104. What was the first thing the rich kid built when he got an erector set for Christmas?

105. What comes around the holidays, is bright and festive and swims in the ocean?

ANSWERS

101. Because he likes to jingle all the weigh
102. Because before Christmas you spend all your green and after Christmas you're in the red
103. Subordinate clauses
104. A tax shelter
105. A Christmas cod

IN THE RED

106. What does "red" mean in Russian?

107. Who was the first play by play announcer to broadcast a televised baseball game?

108. Why were old schoolhouses painted red?

109. Is the Red Sea red?

110. We're a bit red in the face to pose this gift of a question from Santa—Who's the publisher of *Stocking Stumpers?*

ANSWERS

106. "Beautiful"- hence, the name Red Square in Moscow
107. Red Barber
108. Elementary- simply because red was the cheapest paint available
109. Yes- Red algae often appears in the sea, coloring it red.
110. The answer is (Did you already look it up on the copyright page?)-
    Red-Letter Press.

A FLOCK OF QUESTIONS

Match the singular animal with its group name.

111. Chicks	a) Pod
112. Ducks	b) Gang
113. Elks	c) Brood
114. Leopards	d) Band
115. Seals	e) Leap
116. Hens	f) Clutch
117. Gorillas	g) Brace

ANSWERS

111. F
112. G
113. B
114. E
115. A
116. C
117. D

ONE OR THE OTHER

118. Which one sings, the male or female robin?
119. What's the most popular cookie flavor, oatmeal or chocolate chip?
120. Which is on an Izod Lacoste polo shirt, an alligator or crocodile?
121. Which is the biggest encyclopedia in the set, the one labeled "S" or the one marked "T"?
122. Were baseball umpires once referred to as "Diamond Dicks" or "Blind Basemen"?

ANSWERS

118. The male
119. Chocolate chip
120. Crocodile
121. "S"
122. Diamond Dicks

MEASURING UP

123. How long is the Statue of Liberty's nose?

   a) 4 feet b) 6 feet c) 10 feet d) 15 feet

124. How many sheets are there in a ream of paper?

125. How long is a fortnight?

126. It's about 272 feet tall, more than 100 feet in circumference and it's the world's largest plant. What's it called?

127. What are the typical dimensions of a credit card?

   a) 4" x 2" b) 3 3/4" x 2 1/8" c) 3 3/8" x 2 1/8" d) 3" x 2"

ANSWERS

123. A
124. 500
125. Two weeks
126. The General Sherman Tree
    (in Sequoia National Park, California)
127. C

POTPOURRI

128. For what movie could you say that Santa Claus won an Academy Award?

129. According to the National Safety Council, what object is most often choked on by Americans?

130. How did red and green become the traditional colors of Christmas?

131. Beet, carrot, celery, parsley, lettuce, watercress, spinach, and tomato are the ingredients used to make what liquid?

132. True or false: George Washington had a parrot named Polly.

ANSWERS

128. *Miracle on 34th Street*, in which Edmund Gwenn won the Oscar for his portrayal of Ol' St. Nick

129. The toothpick

130. In early times, Christmas tree decorations consisted of red apples on the green tree.

131. They are the eight ingredients in V-8 Juice.

132. True

THE THIRD DEGREE

133. What's the average temperature at Santa's place, the North Pole?
    a) 11 degrees F   b) 1 degree F   c) -11 degrees F   d) -21 degrees F

134. Who's the only United States president to have a PhD?

135. What's the only temperature at which Fahrenheit and Celsius thermometers register the same?

ANSWERS

133. D
134. Woodrow Wilson
135. 40 degrees below zero

TEASER TIMEOUT #2

Once again, it's time to take a trivia breather.
See if you can solve these "familial" brain teasers.

136. Bernetta the St. Bernard is top dog at the North Pole. She had three puppies. Two of them were named Moe and Larry. What was the third puppy's name.

137. It's a little known fact that Donder and Blitzen were born the same day-to the same parents. They look exactly alike and yet they are not twins. How's that possible?

138. She's your uncle's sister but she isn't legally your aunt. Who can she be?

139. Tom's mother had three children. One was named Penny and another named Nickel. What was the name of the third child?

140. Is it legal to marry your widow's sister?

ANSWERS

136. "What" (Notice that there is no question mark after the statement.)

137. They are two of a set of triplets.

138. Your mother

139. Tom, of course

140. Not over your dead body!

INITIALLY SPEAKING

Do you know what these acronyms stand for?

141. CAT (scan)
142. WOMBAT
143. NABISCO
144. LASER
145. KISS

ANSWERS

141. Computerized Axial Tomography

142. Waste of Money, Brains, and Time

143. NAtional BIscuit COmpany

144. Light Amplification by Stimulated Emission
    of Radiation

145. Keep It Simple Stupid

YULETIDE TRIVIA

146. In the Christmas carol *The Twelve Days of Christmas*, what is the fourth day's gift?

147. Who named the Chipmunks in their 1958 *Christmas Song*?

148. What do Little Richard, Barbara Mandrell and Sissy Spacek share in common?

149. *Auld Lang Syne* is a favorite of Santa's. Just what does "auld lang syne" mean?

150. Who invented Christmas tree lights?
     a) Elisha Gray b) Thomas Edison c) Edward Johnson d) Magic Johnson

ANSWERS

146. If you said "4 calling birds", you're wrong. They are "collied" birds (black birds). Oh, and about the fifth day's gift- the five golden rings are ringed pheasants, not jewelry.

147. Performer and songwriter David Seville. Alvin and Simon were named for two executives at Liberty Records, Al Bennett and Simon Waronker. Theodore was named for the recording engineer, Ted Keep.

148. They share the same birthday- Christmas.

149. It's Scottish for "old long ago".

150. C (He was Edison's partner. Johnson hung the first string of lights on his tree in 1882.)

THE NAME GAME

151. According to the Boat Owners Association of the U.S., what is the most popular name given to boats?

152. What is Paul McCartney's first name?

153. It was originally called Wired Radio Inc., but you know it better by what name?

154. What were the nicknames of Old West outlaws Robert Parker and Harry Longabaugh?

155. Organized crime is called Yakuza in this country.
Where in the world is this?

ANSWERS

151. Odyssey
152. James
153. Muzak
154. Butch Cassidy and the Sundance Kid
155. Japan

FUN 'N' GAMES

156. How many holes are there on a Chinese checkerboard?

157. According to the directions, whose murder are you solving when you play a game of Clue?

158. Ole Kirk Christiansen qualifies as one of Santa's biggest helpers on his block. Why?

159. How many squares are on a Scrabble board?

160. In the game of Yahtzee, how many points is a full house worth?

ANSWERS

156. 121
157. Mr. Boddy's
158. He invented LEGOS.
159. 225
160. 25

PRESIDENTIAL PAIRS

161. Who are the two U.S. presidents to have won the Nobel Peace Prize?

162. Name the two presidents buried at Arlington National Cemetery.

163. Two U.S. presidents were so popular that no one ran against them. One was George Washington. Can you come up with the other?

164. What two presidents died the same day?

165. Who were the only grandfather and grandson to serve as president?

ANSWERS

161. Theodore Roosevelt and Woodrow Wilson

162. John F. Kennedy and William Howard Taft

163. James Monroe, in 1820- no one ran against him as that time was called "the era of good feeling."

164. John Adams and Thomas Jefferson, coincidentally, died on the same day and, coincidence of coincidences, they died on the Fourth of July, 1826.

165. William Henry Harrison and Benjamin Harrison

PHRASE CRAZE

See if you can figure out what items these phrases represent.

166. <u>MIND</u>
      MATTER

167. W   S
        O   D
          R
        O   D
      W   S

168. CCCCCCC

169. THENIGHT CHRISTMAS

170. STAND   TAKE   TO   TAKING
       I   YOU   THROW   MY

ANSWERS

166. Mind over matter (Fact: One of the greatest minds of all time, Albert Einstein, was offered the presidency of Israel in 1952 but turned it down saying, "I know a little about nature, and hardly anything about men.")

167. Crosswords (Fact: Newspaper editor Arthur Wynne published the first crossword puzzle in America in the *New York World* on December 21, 1913.)

168. The Seven Seas (Fact: There are no specific "seven seas". It is an expression meaning all the oceans and seas of the world.)

169. The Night Before Christmas (Fact: *'Twas the Night Before Christmas*, by Clement Clark Moore, was originally titled *A Visit From St. Nicholas*.)

170. I Understand You Undertake to Overthrow My Undertaking (Fact: Speaking of undertakers, did you know that during Civil War times, they were referred to as "Doctor"?)

TRANSATLANTIC TRANSLATION

Travelling the world over as he does, Santa has to get by in any tongue but he sometimes gets confused between the way English is spoken in Britain and the way it's said in the U.S. See if you can match up the American word with the English term for it.

171. eggplant	a) larder
172. diaper	b) truncheon
173. parka	c) waistcoat
174. cream of wheat	d) aubergine
175. pantry	e) nappy
176. vest	f) semolina
177. nightstick	g) anorak

ANSWERS

171. D
172. E
173. G
174. F
175. A
176. C
177. B

COAST TO COAST

178. What state's coastline is longer than that of all of the other states' coastlines combined in the United States?

179. What organization was originally called the Revenue Marine Service?

180. What is the only Great Lake whose coastline is entirely in the U.S.?

181. This may prove to be a thorn in your side- Can you name the singing group that had a hit single called *Poison Ivy*?

182. Santa thinks there's a 99-44/100% chance you won't get this one. Can you name the west African republic whose capital is Abidjan?

ANSWERS

178. Alaska
179. The United States Coast Guard
180. Lake Michigan
181. The Coasters
182. Ivory Coast

TRUE OR FALSE

183. Banana oil comes from lemons.

184. The Holland Tunnel, connecting New York City and New Jersey under the Hudson River, is named after the nationality of Manhattan's first colonists.

185. Columbia, Harvard, Yale and Princeton were the original four schools in a college athletic league. The Roman numeral for four is IV so they decided to call themselves the "Ivy" League.

186. The weight of whales is measured on a Saffin-Simpson scale.

187. Polar bears can outrun reindeer- even Santa's!

ANSWERS

183. False- but it doesn't come from bananas either. It's an artificial mixture which smells like bananas.

184. False- it's named after the engineer who directed the tunnel-building operation, Clifford Milburn Holland.

185. True

186. False- If you missed this one it's a real natural disaster. Hurricanes are measured on the Saffin-Simpson scale. (By the way, the Moby Dicks of the world are sized up at whale-weigh stations. Ho! Ho! Ho!)

187. True

TRIVIQUATION

Test your math and your trivia wits here. Fill in the number portion of the answers suggested by the clues and then perform the arithmetic to solve the triviquation.

188. Number of black keys on a piano ...._____

189. Number of U.S. presidents who have
     shared the first name James...x_____

190. The retired uniform number of Yogi Berra and Bill Dickey .....-_____

191. Santa's total number of reindeer ....-_____

192. Words in English language that have 3 consecutive
     double-letters..+_____

193. Laps in Indianapolis 500 ....=_____

ANSWERS

188. 36
189. 6 (Buchanan, Carter, Garfield, Madison, Monroe and Polk)
190. 8
191. 9 (You didn't forget Rudolph, did you?)
192. 1 (bookkeeper)
193. 200

HARDBALL TRIVIA

194. "Small bowls" was a popular game among the likes of Thomas Jefferson and John Adams. By what name do we know "small bowls" today?

195. In billiards, are the low-numbered balls solid or striped?

196. Umpires rub up baseballs before games with what substance?

197. What two sporting balls have a maximum allowable weight of 256 ounces?

ANSWERS

194. Marbles
195. Solid
196. Baltimore clay
197. A bowling ball and a shotput

LOONY LAWS

Our lawmakers have handed us some pretty silly regulations over the years. See if you can tell which of the following laws are, or were, true- and which are false.

198. It's against the law for a woman of "notorious bad character" to ride a horse through the streets of Columbia, S.C.

199. In Quitman, Georgia, it is illegal for a chicken to cross the road.

200. It's illegal to carry ice cream cones in your pocket in Lexington, Kentucky.

201. In Cheapside, Texas, lawyers are bound by legislation to accept minimum wage fees.

ANSWERS

198. True

199. True

200. True

201. False- but there really is a Cheapside, Texas (And this question reminded Santa of an old joke: A guy goes into a lawyer's office and says, "How much do you charge?" The lawyer responds, "Two hundred dollars for three questions." Then the guy says, "That's a lot of money, isn't it?" And the lawyer answers, "Yes. What's your final question?"

    Oh, and one other thing: Did you know that Mrs. Claus fancies herself as an attorney? You can, too. Fact is, anyone can act on someone's behalf and be called their attorney but to be called a lawyer you must be a graduate of law school.)

SPORTS SHORTS

202. Why is the playing field of a Rio de Janiero soccer stadium surrounded by a moat?

203. What all-around athletic great had a twin brother who died of pneumonia at the age of eight?

204. A sport called "poona" originated in India. What is it known as today?

205. Composer Albert von Tilzer wrote *Take Me Out to the Ball Game* in 1908. What was odd about this?

206. Who invented the national game of Canada- lacrosse?

ANSWERS

202. To keep overzealous fans from spilling out on to the field
203. Jim Thorpe
204. Badminton
205. He had never been to a baseball game and would not see one until some twenty years after he wrote the song.
206. American Indians

HOLIDAY HO HOs #2

Santa's sidekick, Henny Elfman, is at it again as we take another timeout from trivia. See if you can answer these Christmas sillies.

207. What does Santa Claus become on Christmas Day?

208. Fill in the punchline: You can tell it's Christmas in the nineties. The shopping mall Santa said to the little girl, "And what would you like for Christmas?"

    She responded, "_____?"

209. What is Santa's favorite state in the U.S.?

210. How do you keep someone on Santa's naughty list in suspense?

ANSWERS

207. A "beatnick"
208. "Didn't you get my fax?"
209. Idaho!Ho!Ho!
210.

TIME AND TIME AGAIN

211. Is Thanksgiving always on the last Thursday of November?

212. What is one-sixtieth of one-sixtieth of one-twentyfourth of a day?

213. True or false: Any month that starts on a Sunday, will have a Friday the 13th.

214. How long is the minute hand on Big Ben?
a) 3 feet b) 5 feet c) 8 feet d) 11 feet

215. Here's a trivia teaser: "Two days ago I was 69 years old. Next year, I'll be 72." How can someone make this statement?

ANSWERS

211. No- it's on the fourth Thursday of the month.

212. One second

213. True

214. Strictly speaking, the answer is "none of the above". Big Ben is the bell inside the clock, not the clock itself. But, 'tis the season, so Santa will give you credit if you answered "d".

215. This can only be said about someone who is born on December 31 and is saying that on January 1.

POTPOURRI

216. Cartoonist Thomas Nast is credited with creating the modern version of Santa Claus. In these days of being politically correct, what two famous animal drawings did he create?

217. The act of snapping one's fingers is called a:
a) fillip   b) bezel   c) callithump   d)haruspex

218. How big is a "two-by-four" piece of wood?

219. All pilots on international flights identify themselves in what language?

220. "Matinees" are generally afternoon events. The word "matinee" is French for what meaning?

ANSWERS

216. The donkey for the Democratic Party and the elephant for the Republicans
217. A
218. 1 1/2 inches by 3 1/2 inches
219. English
220. Morning

MY WORD!

221. What is alphabetically unique about the words unnoticeably, uncomplimentary, and subcontinental?

222. What is a capitonym?

223. Can you name a seven letter word with three U's in it that's unusual?

224. What odd trait does the word "clip" have?

225. There are only three words in the English language which end in "ceed." Can you name them?

ANSWERS

221. They each contain all the vowels in reverse order.

222. It is a word that takes on a new meaning when capitalized- polish and Polish, for example.

223. Unusual

224. It has opposite meanings- to clasp together, and to cut apart.

225. Exceed, proceed, and succeed

MOTHERS OF INVENTION

Match the inventor with the better mousetrap.

226. Mary Anderson   a) mini-skirt
227. Ruth Wakefield   b) windshield wiper
228. Granny Smith   c) chocolate chip cookies
229. Mary Quant   d) green apples

ANSWERS

226. B, in 1902
227. C, in 1933
228. D, in 1868 (in Australia)
229. A, in 1965

TRIVIQUATION #2

Once again, fill in the number portion of the answers suggested by the clues and then do the math to solve the puzzle.

230. Number of toes on a pig's foot .... _____

231. Spaces on a Monopoly board .... x _____

232. Ridges around the edge of a dime .... - _____

233. Hexagon sides .... ÷ _____

234. The sum of opposite sides of a dice cube .... - _____

235. Number of children of the "Father of our Country" ..... = _____

ANSWERS

230. 4
231. 40
232. 118
233. 6
234. 7
235. George Washington had no children.

THE ALMIGHTY DOLLAR

236. The one dollar bill is the most frequently circulated paper currency in the U.S.? What's second?

237. What would you have if your Aunt Lizzie sent you a pocket-sized copy of John Trumbull's depiction of *The Signing of the Declaration of Independence* for Christmas?

238. What's the largest amount of money in coins you could have without being able to make change for a dollar? (Not to remind you of January's bills or anything...)

239. Whose portrait is on the $50 bill and, for an extra helping of plum pudding, what building is pictured on the flip side?

240. What famous Christmas story begins with the line, "One dollar and eighty-seven cents"?

ANSWERS

236. The $20 bill

237. You'd have two bucks. It's on the back of the $2 bill.

238. $1.19 (three quarters, three dimes and four pennies)

239. U.S. Grant is on the front, the U.S. Capitol building is on the back

240. *The Gift of the Magi* (As this O. Henry story goes, that was all the money Jim Young had with which to buy a Christmas gift for his wife, Delia.)

PHRASE CRAZE #2

Here are some more trivial messages that Santa's elves scrawled on the frosted workshop windows for you to solve.

241.
```
            l
        a       a
      m           m
     i             i
      c           c
       e         e
        d       d
```

242. PE/A
SOUP

243. gsge

244. /R/E/A/D/I/N/G/

245. ABCDEFGHIJKMNOPQRSTUVWXYZ

ANSWERS

241. Decimal point (Fact: You probably know that the James Bond "007" books were written by Ian Fleming, but did you know that there was a .007 story which was not written by Fleming, but by Rudyard Kipling? Notice the decimal point.)

242. Split pea soup (Fact: Regarding soup, bird's nest soup really is from a bird's nest. In China, this delicacy is made from the Asian swift's nest.)

243. Scrambled eggs (Fact: *Scrambled Eggs* was the original title for the Beatles' hit song *Yesterday.*)

244. Reading between the lines (Fact: Thomas Edison preferred Braille in reading.)

245. Noel (Look between the K and the M- which brings us to another fact: KLM, the Dutch airline, is an acronym for Koninklijke-Luchtvaart-Maatschappij. Operating since 1919, it is the oldest airline in the world today.)

LAST CALL

246. In *The Wizard of Oz*, what is Dorothy's last name?

247. Whose last words were, "How were the circus receipts tonight at Madison Square Garden?"

248. What is telosphobia?

249. Zythum is a malt beverage brewed by the ancient Egyptians. Of what other distinction is zythum?

250. What was the last name of Virginia, the eight year old who wrote to the *New York Sun* and asked if there really was a Santa Claus?

ANSWERS

246. Gale

247. Circus showman P.T. Barnum (1810-1891)

248. A fear of being last

249. It's the last word in many unabridged English dictionaries.

250. O'Hanlon- and, as the editor of the paper wrote back, "Yes, Virginia. There is a Santa Claus." Merry Christmas!